CONTENTS

PART I

PART II

PREFACE

PART 1

From Part 1, First Chapter to Sixth Chapter discusses about Major division of Medical Electronic Equipment, Life Cycle of a Product, Various divisions of Start Up, Various Channels to Start a Proprietor Company, Essential Steps for a Business Start Up, Steps needed to set up your Business.

From Chapter Seven to Thirteen discusses Revenue Generation in Proprietorship Company, Conversion of Proprietor to Start Up and about generating revenue for the Start Up.

Further, it discusses about the Licenses required to Import and Export and to Construct/Import the Medical Equipments. Also, it discusses about Pitching to the Investors and to the Competitions.

PART 2

Tis part discusses about Necessary Legal Documents for Start Up, LLP, Limitations of LLP, LLP Vs Partnership, Required Compliance of LLP and Start Up, Make in India, Financial Support to Start Up, Start Up India Seed fund and about Blessed Messenger and Wander Capatilists.

Also, we have published 3 companies' Interview about their experience in Launching Start Up in India.

Dr. S.Saravanan, B.Sc., AMIE., ME., Phd.,

Dr. C.Umayal, ME., Phd.,

Mr. K. Krishanakumar, M.Sc., MBA.,

Er. Nadipelli Adithi Rao, BE.,

ACKNOWLEDGEMENT

Dedicated to my Parents and Guruji who taught me from LKG to PhD.

I thank Mr. Raghavendra Prasad who was my colleague in Instruments and Machines Incorporated, Chennai, for his personnel guidance in Marketing the Medical Electronic Equipment's. I thank Late Mr. C.Dayakar Reddy who has given opportunity to market Indigenous Medical Equipment's in Salem, Erode and Coimbatore Area

After 12 years experience in Marketing Medical Equipment, I came to Academic Side working in various Engineering Colleges and upgraded myself to ME., (Medical Electronics – College of Engineering, Guindy) and Phd., (Medical Electronics – Sathyabama University, Chennai) in Part Time. I came out of Faculty position and started Proprietorship Company, SMK Instruments and Machines Incorporated in the year of 2014.

Mr.C.P. Velusami, Managing Director, Kody Tech Ltd., and Kody Medical Electronics Pvt Ltd., is the first person in India to bring maximum NRI shares to TamilNadu Hospitals Pvt Ltd. With his guidance, I have taken dealership of Bio Radio from Neuro Technologies Pvt Ltd from the USA. I had 5 major installations:

1. SSN College of Engineering, Chennai
2. IIT, Bhubaneshwar
3. IIT, Gujarat
4. IIT, Patna and
5. GH Patel College of Engineering and Technology, Gujarat

When I expanded Proprietorship Company to Xerion Labs Healthcare Solutions Pvt Ltd., I got funds from IVP through Ganesan Incubation and Entrepreneurial Center and developed Prototype of PREDVITTAL24 which needed upgradation and due to my ill health, I closed down my operations of Xerion Labs Healthcare Solutions Pvt Ltd., and now focusing on writing books technically about the Medical Electronic products and in general topic.

I strongly believe and advice students to work as a marketing person for one year, to understand the customer needs and then becoming R&D or Quality Control or any other specialization to start a Start Up.

Instead of working only as a faculty or an Industry person, if there is a category who has changed from industry to faculty or faculty to industry, that experience is valid to develop the product.

I thank Dr.C. Umayal and also Mr. K. Krishnakumar who was my Managing Director of Xerion Labs Healthcare Solutions Pvt Ltd, for Co-authoring this text book.

I thank Er. Nadipellii Adithi Rao for her work in Proof Reading, Marketing etc., of this work.

I thank Ms. Manoramya for her beautiful design of the Cover page of this book.

I thank Ms. Sangeetha, Proprietrix, J.M. Enterprises, Ammapet for her formatting work of this text book.

Dr. S.SARAVANAN

GeneAura Private Limited

CIN NO: U85100TN2021PTC141786

1. How We Got the Idea for Our Project?

Geneaura was founded with a mission to make genetic testing more accessible and to educate people about the importance of understanding their genetic health. While genetics plays a crucial role in diagnosing and managing various conditions, there was a gap in awareness and accessibility. The goal was simple help individuals make informed health decisions through personalized genetic insights. The idea for GeneAura was born out of a deep realization that healthcare needed a shift from a reactive approach to a proactive one. We saw firsthand how people struggled with lifestyle disorders, unexplained infertility, and metabolic conditions often receiving generalized treatments that didn't consider their unique genetic makeup.

With advancements in genomics, we recognized an opportunity to empower individuals with personalized health insights. Our vision was clear

- To make genetic testing and counseling accessible, helping people make informed decisions about their health, nutrition, and well-being.
- GeneAura was created to bridge the gap between complex genetic science and practical, everyday health solutions.

2. How We Got Funds?

GeneAura started as a self-funded venture We invested our own resources to build the foundation covering research, setting up operations, and developing partnerships Instead of relying on external investors initially, we focused on generating revenue through our services, reinvesting profits to scale and improve our offerings. Strategic collaborations with healthcare institutions, clinics, and wellness centers helped us grow without depending on large capital injections. Our business model was designed for sustainability, ensuring that we could expand without compromising quality

3. How We Chose Our Mentor?

We didn't have a mentor. Instead, we became our own mentors, learning everything through experience, research, and continuous adaptation. From understanding the complexities of genetic testing to navigating the business landscape, we relied on our ability to analyze challenges, seek knowledge, and make informed decisions. Rather than following a pre-set path, we created our own, setting the right direction for GeneAura. Every challenge was a learning opportunity, and every milestone was a testament to our ability to grow independently.

Dr.Dakshina Moorthy Janani
GeneAura Private Limited,
Chennai

📞 +91 8248408851 ✉ care@geneaura.com 📍 No: 2/6 , 4th Street , Sakthi Nagar , Choolaimedu , Chennai -94 🌐 www.geneaura.com

Genetic Counselling I Genetic Testing I Genetic Report Interpretation I Nutrigenomics I Pharmacogenomics I PCOS Management

4. What are the challenges you met in the Start up Journey?

Starting GeneAura was not easy. We faced multiple challenges, including:

- **Building Awareness** - Genetic testing is still an emerging field, and educating both consumers and healthcare providers about its benefits required persistent effort.
- **Regulatory & Ethical Compliance** - Understanding and adhering to legal requirements, patient data privacy laws, and ethical guidelines was a complex but crucial process.
- **Financial & Operational Management** - Running a genomics company requires high investment in sequencing technology and bioinformatics. We optimized costs through strategic partnerships with labs and efficient workflow management.
- **Competition & Market Positioning** - Differentiating ourselves in a growing but competitive industry meant focusing on quality, personalized services, and in-depth genetic counseling rather than just selling test reports.
- **Scaling the Business** - Expanding our services, building the right team, and ensuring operational efficiency required continuous effort and innovation.

5. How We Established the Company?

Geneaura was built step by step starting with genetic counseling and testing, then expanding into wellness services. We registered the company with a strong ethical foundation, ensuring compliance with healthcare standards. GeneAura was built on the foundation of scientific expertise, resilience, and a strong commitment to precision healthcare. Here's how we made it happen

- We legally established GeneAura, setting up operations with a clear focus on clinical and wellness genomics
- Instead of relying on external guidance, we gathered a team of experts in genetics, bioinformatics, and healthcare to drive our vision forward.
- Our focus was on clinical genetic testing, wellness genomics, reproductive health, and personalized nutrition ensuring our tests provided actionable insights.
- We partnered with hospitals, wellness clinics, and healthcare providers to expand our reach and integrate genomics into routine medical practice.
- Through seminars, social media engagement, and medical collaborations, we actively educated people about the power of genetic testing.
- By carefully balancing investment and revenue, we ensured GeneAura's financial stability while continuously upgrading our technology and services.

Education and awareness were key to our growth. We invested in outreach programs, workshops, and social media campaigns to help people understand why genetic testing matters. With time, our impact grew, and today, GeneAura stands as a testament to the power of self-learning, determination, and innovation. Without a mentor or external hand-holding, we built a genomics company that is shaping the future of personalized healthcare. Our journey has just begun, and we are committed to pushing the boundaries of what's possible in genetic science for better health outcomes

Dr.Dakshina Moorthy Janani
GeneAura Private Limited,
Chennai

1. Therapeutic and Diagnostic Equipment

In the field of medical electronics, therapeutic and diagnostic devices have different functions, each essential to the provision of health care.

1.1   Therapeutic Devices

Therapeutic devices are created to address medical issues by delivering different forms of energy or treatments directly to the patient. These tools are utilized to provide therapy or care, with the goal of reducing symptoms or curing ailments. Examples are: Surgical Tools: Instruments such as scalpels, forceps,

and surgical cauterizers are employed in surgeries to cut, dissect, or coagulate tissue.

Implants: Devices such as pacemakers and artificial joints are surgically inserted to restore or enhance bodily functions.

Dialysis Equipment: Machines that purify blood for individuals suffering from kidney failure.

Defibrillators: Devices that reinstate a regular heartbeat by administering electrical shocks.

Therapeutic devices generally convert electrical energy into other forms, such as mechanical, thermal, or radiative energy, to produce therapeutic outcomes.

1.2   Diagnostic Devices:

Conversely, diagnostic devices are employed to identify and diagnose medical issues. These tools assist healthcare providers in determining the underlying causes of symptoms or illnesses by tracking and assessing various physiological indicators. Examples of such devices include:

<u>Imaging equipment:</u> X-rays, MRI scans, and CT scans generate pictures of internal bodily structures.

<u>Stethoscopes:</u> Utilized for hearing internal body sounds.

<u>Electrocardiograms (ECGs):</u> Assess the heart's electrical activity.

<u>Blood Pressure Monitors:</u> Evaluate blood pressure.

Diagnostic tools can vary from basic items like thermometers to sophisticated imaging technologies such as MRI machines.

1.3   Key Differences

<u>Purpose:</u> Therapeutic devices are intended for treatment, whereas diagnostic devices are meant for diagnosing conditions.

<u>Functionality:</u> Therapeutic instruments deliver energy or interventions to address medical issues, while diagnostic tools evaluate and track physiological metrics to support diagnosis.

Examples: Examples of therapeutic equipment include pacemakers and dialysis machines, while examples of diagnostic equipment consist of MRI machines and stethoscopes.

In conclusion, therapeutic devices concentrate on managing medical issues, while diagnostic tools are used to identify and evaluate those issues. Both types of equipment play a crucial role in healthcare in order to provide thorough patient care.

2. Life Cycle of a Product

A medical electronic product life cycle management ensures safety, regulatory compliance and market readiness through a structured series of phases. Below is a detailed breakdown of the key stages. The product design phase is the initial stage where the specifications of the medical electronic product are determined based on the physician's recommendations and user requirements. The design should consider factors like sensitivity, accuracy, patient comfort, and durability.

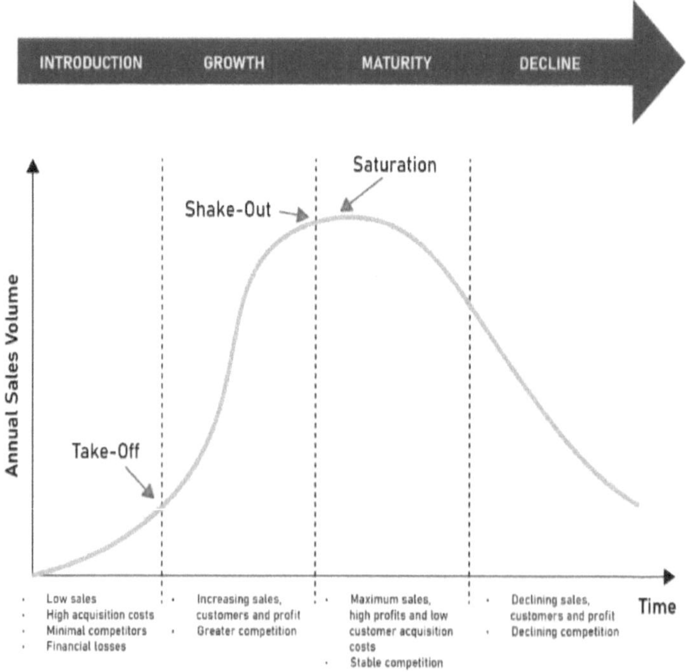

Electrical components like microcontrollers, sensors, and batteries are selected and integrated into the device. Prototyping follows, with the verification of electrical connections, wiring, and performance parameters. Stakeholders review the design for usability, safety, and manufacturability. Once approved, mass production can begin.

In the component procurement phase, suppliers are vetted,

and components are purchased. Strict control is maintained over component specifications to ensure they meet quality and safety standards. Libraries and sources are established for future reference and repairs. Assembly operations break down the components into sub-assemblies and perform the final integration of the device.

Clear work instructions and quality control standards are implemented to ensure consistency and completeness.

Assembly defects or non-conforming products are identified and eliminated or resolved before final assembly.

The testing phase includes rigorous quality control checks. Functional tests verify the device's sensitivity, accuracy, and response time. Reliability tests ensure the device can withstand varied conditions (e.g., temperature, humidity) without failing.

Safety tests, such as electrical safety certifications (UL, ISO), are conducted to guarantee patient safety. Inspections and tests are documented for traceability and compliance purposes. After successful testing, the final inspection step is taken.

Here, a random sample of products is examined for conformity with initial specifications, technical drawings, and quality standards. Any remaining defects are identified and resolved. Once passed, the products are ready for packaging and preparation for logistics.

The packaging operation ensures each unit is packed properly with necessary accessories and information (e.g., instruction manuals, sterilization certificates). The packed products are stored in controlled environments to prevent damage or degradation until the shipment process begins.

Logistics and distribution manage the transportation of products to distribution centers, hospitals, and clinical settings. Order processing, shipment tracking, and inventory management systems are implemented to ensure timely delivery to customers or healthcare institutions.

The product is launched into the market once it has passed all quality controls and is available for purchase or distribution by healthcare companies or providers. Marketing efforts provide product details, patient instructions, and feedback for a successful launch. Post-launch monitoring includes gathering patient outcomes, side effects, and medical implications through cooperative relationships with healthcare professionals. Field reports are analyzed to identify improvements, which can lead to design revisions or recalls if necessary.

The product's life cycle continues with ongoing support, maintenance, and retirement or end-of-life planning based on obsolescence, regulatory changes, or resource availability.

By following this life cycle management approach, manufacturers can ensure the safety, effectiveness, and longevity of medical electronic products, meeting the needs of healthcare professionals and patients. This methodical process allows for continuous improvement, sustainability, and confidence in the devices used to save lives and improve healthcare outcomes. The life cycle to manufacture a medical electronic product involves a series of phases to ensure safety, regulatory compliance and market readiness. Below is a detailed breakdown of the key stages.

2.1 Concept Phase Objective:

Develop the initial idea and assess feasibility. The device concept is conceived, focusing on solving a medical need. Market analysis and technical feasibility studies are conducted. Prototypes may be created to validate core functionality.

2.2 Planning Phase Objective:

Define requirements and regulatory strategy. User needs are translated into technical specifications. Regulatory requirements (e.g., FDA, CE marking) and risk classification are established. Resource allocation, timelines, and cost estimates are finalized

2.3 Design & Development Phase Objective:

Create detailed designs and prototypes. Engineers develop iterative designs, incorporating electrical safety, biocompatibility, and usability. Design verification (meeting specifications) and validation (meeting user needs) are performed. Risk management plans are drafted to address potential hazards.

2.4 Validation Phase

Objective: Practice safety and efficacy before production.

Process Validation: IQ (Installation Qualification), OQ (Operational Qualification), and PQ (Performance Qualification) guarantee repeating of manufacturing.

Clinical Evaluation: Real life tests to validate the effectiveness. Regulatory submissions (e.g., FDA 510(k), CE marking) are prepared.

Technology Transfer & Manufacturing Objective: Transition from design to mass production.

Knowledge transfer occurs between design and manufacturing teams.
Production processes are validated, and quality control systems (e.g., ISO 13485) are implemented.
Pilot runs and scalability assessments ensure manufacturing readiness
Launch Phase Objective: Introduce the product to the market. Training and support materials are provided to healthcare providers. Marketing and distribution channels are activated.
Post-Market Surveillance Objective: Monitor performance and

address issues.

Post-Market Surveillance (PMS): Track adverse events and customer feedback.

2.5 Continuous Improvement:

Design or manufacturing updates implemented based on data. Compliance with standards like ISO 13485:2016 guarantees the ongoing quality of the product. Key Considerations for Electronic Medical Devices.

Electrical Safety: Extensive testing for EMC emissions and electrical insulation of the final product.

Data Security: Applicability to GDPR or HIPAA (in USA) and in India CEDESCO for devices that deal with patient data.

2.6 Supply Chain: Reliable Components and Traceability:

This way, through this life cycle, innovation is in harmony with regulation while manufacturers are able to provide safe and effective medical electronic products to market.

3. Taxonomy of Startup in India:

3.1 Different Types of Startups:

1. Scalable Startups: A scalable startup is a type of business model that is planned to have a rapid growth and expansion and is usually backed by new innovations and strategic investments. Such startups are designed to become very profitable through the use of technology and good planning.

Key Characteristics:
- Designed to expand quickly through technology and automation.
- Attracts venture capital or angel investment for growth.
- Focuses on a unique, innovative product or service.
- Operates with a goal of market dominance and significant revenue generation.

Advantages:
- High potential for growth and profitability.
- Ability to reach a global market.
- Attracts strong investor interest due to growth potential.
- Generates employment and drives economic development.

2. Small Business Startups:
- Operated by individuals or families.
- Primarily serves local communities
- Limited investment requirements.
- Growth is steady but not necessarily rapid.

3. Social Startups:
- Focus on solving societal or environmental issues.
- Operate as non-profits or social enterprises.
- Aim for sustainability rather than maximizing profit.

4. Large Business Startups:
- Often created by established corporations.
- Enter new markets with innovative solutions.
- Require substantial investment and R&D.

5. Lifestyle Startups:
- Built around the founders' passion or hobbies.
- Examples include content creators, artists, and niche businesses.
- Typically self-funded and focused on personal fulfillment rather than rapid scaling.

6. Buyable Startups:
- Created with the intention of being acquired by a larger company.
- Common in tech industries where bigger firms acquire smaller innovative startups.

These startup categories reflect India's diverse entrepreneurial landscape, with opportunities for businesses of all scales and sectors to thrive.

3.1.1 Scalable Startups: Characteristics and Benefits

Key Characteristics of Scalable Startups:
1. Innovative Solutions – Such startups offer new and unique products or services that solve specific problems and may create new markets.
2. Scalable Business Model – Growth is sustainable and does not happen with a corresponding increase in costs.
3. Investment Support – External funding from venture capitalists and angel investors is an important part of their growth.
4. Technology Integration – The use of technology enhances the performance of the organization and makes it more efficient and scalable.
5. High Market Potential – Such startups are aimed at growing industries and have a large number of potential customers.

Benefits of Scalable Startups
1. Fast Growth – They can grow fast and become the market leaders in their niches.

2.   Competitive Advantage – Their innovation strategy makes it hard for other companies to emulate their success.
3.   Investor Interest – High growth rates are interesting to investors who want to get high returns on their investment.
4.   Job Creation – As they expand, they create employment, which is useful for the economy.
5.   Entrepreneurial Satisfaction – The founders feel fulfilled developing important and successful enterprises.
6.   Startup companies are designed for quick growth and profitability and are scalable, based on technology and good business models and investor backing.

3.1.2 Understanding of Small Business Startups

A small business startup is between traditional small businesses and early stage startups. Here's how they compare:

<u>Small Business Features</u>
- Definition: Based on employee count and revenue, for instance, in the U.S., businesses are considered small if they have less than 500 employees and annual revenue of less than
- $7.5 million for non manufacturing sectors.
- Key Traits: Function in known markets, concentrate on achieving financial stability and are usually owned independently.
- Funding Sources: The usual sources of funding include the owner's savings, banks or other traditional lenders, and alternative financing.

<u>Startup Features</u>
- Definition: A company that concentrates on creating a new product or service and identifying a growth strategy with the potential for scalability.
- Key Traits: Needs a lot of capital, many times operates at a loss in the first years, and seeks to replace or create markets.
- Funding Sources: They are often funded by venture capital firms due to the companies' potential for rapid growth.

<u>How Small Business Startups Differ</u>

Concept: Means new small businesses in the early stage. Although they have some startup features, they pay much more attention to the stability than to the rapid growth.

Growth Approach: They do not seek to become scalable startups and therefore do not seek venture capital funding; instead, they seek sustainable, steady revenue growth.

A small business startup focuses on long term sustainability and profitability as opposed to aggressive market disruption.

3.1.3 What is a Lifestyle Business and How Does it Relate to Startups?

The term "Lifestyle Startup" is not well understood since it combines the ideas of lifestyle businesses and startups.

However, they have different intentions.

<u>What is a Lifestyle Business?</u>

Definition: A business owned by an entrepreneur to enable him or her lead the kind of life he or she wants to live without necessarily focusing on making profits.

Key Features:

- ✓ Flexible Operations – The owners of the business are able to work when they want and where they want to work.

- ✓ Limited Scalability – Growth is usually sustainable and moderate and not rapid.

- ✓ Self-Funded – Most are owned by personal funds or small business loans.

- ✓ Purpose-Driven – The concentration is on producing a reasonable return instead of growth through aggressive expansion.

Lifestyle businesses help entrepreneurs to be able to earn a healthy income without compromising on the quality of life that they want to lead.

3.1.4 Startup

A start up is a new enterprise that focuses on growth and scale up. Many such ventures need outside funding to realize their ambitions.

Key Characteristics
- Rapid Growth: The single most important goal is to grow fast.
- External Funding: Some but not all require funding from third parties, such as venture capitalists or angel investors.
- Scalability: Intended to grow very large in a short period of time.
- Market Disruption: May seek to disrupt markets or achieve a significant financial milestone such as an acquisition or initial public offering (IPO).

The term 'lifestyle startup' is sometimes used to describe a business model that combines the best of both worlds – flexibility and growth. However, this term is not used extensively in business literature and is actually a combination of two concepts.

Some of the most common lifestyle business ideas include

More and more lifestyle businesses are emerging for example

By 2025, AI, green technology, and digital education are expected to emerge as major industry sectors that could generate business for both lifestyle businesses and startups.

3.1.5 Buyable Startups

A buyable startup is a type of business that is started with the plan of being bought by another company. Such startups are usually founded to create new products or offer new services that could be interesting to the big players in the industry.

Key Characteristics:
- Exit Oriented: Long term plan is not to be independent but to be profitable.
- Industry Focus: Most common in technology, software and mobile application.
- Innovation Driven: Come up with solutions that are relevant to the market or that can add value to other large organizations.
- Funding Sources: The founders, credit lines or small amounts of money from investors.
- Acquisition Strategy: Founded with the understanding of being acquired by a established company.
- Growth Pattern: Early stage growth is rapid and then levels off after the acquisition.

Benefits:
- For Entrepreneurs: A well defined exit plan is a way of getting a return on investment and work, and the buyouts are usually between $5 million and $50 million.
- For Acquiring Companies: A way to obtain new technologies, knowledge, and talented employees.
- Notable Acquisitions
- Instagram & WhatsApp (Acquired by Facebook)
- Whole Foods (Acquired by Amazon)
- Postmates (Acquired by Uber)
- Nest (Acquired by Google).

3.1.6 Big Business Startups

A big business startup or, alternatively, an offshoot startup is the term denoted to new ventures which are created by

established companies in order to venture into new markets or create new products. Such companies are not completely independent startups; they are assisted by the parent company's financial and moral support.

Key Characteristics
- Corporate Backing: Backed by a large organization with

strong financial standing.
- Innovation & Expansion: Seeks to introduce new services or products in undiscoved markets.
- Competitive Advantage: Supports from the parent company's facilities and customer base.

Examples

Corporations such as Apple and Google are known to establish in-house startups in order to research on new technologies or new industries in a bid to stay ahead of the competition and to build new businesses.

Big business startups are distinct from the normal startups because they are a part of the existing organizations rather than separate entities.

3.1.7 Social Startups

A social startup is a kind of business which is established to achieve certain social, cultural, or environmental objectives and at the same time the company has to meet its financial goals.

Unlike other startups, such businesses are more oriented towards the benefit of society.

Key Characteristics
- Purpose-Driven: Designs to provide practical solutions with environmentally friendly business plans.
- Scalability: Intended for long-term growth while maintaining the social mission.
- For-Profit or Non-Profit Models: Runs on one or the other structure based on the goal.

These ventures are, therefore, examples of what can be achieved when ideas are combined with social responsibility to effect change in different areas of life.

Key Characteristics of Social Startups:

- Mission-Driven: The primary goal is to address social, environmental, or cultural issues rather than maximizing profits.

- Innovative Solutions: Startups develop and implement new strategies to address root causes of a problem, which can involve the use of technology or new business strategies.
- Market-Oriented: Although they give priority to the social results, they function within the market system in order to ensure that they are able to finance their activities.
- Types: Social startups are classified into different categories, including leveraged non-profits, hybrid non-profits, and social business ventures.
- Examples of Social Startups:
- Healthcare: Projects aimed at designing low-cost medical devices or improving the availability of healthcare to people in need.
- Education: Activities that are directed at offering learning resources and solutions to people who cannot afford it.

Environment: Organizations that are involved in sustainable energy, waste management, and other environmental activities.

Social startups are also known to be the solution providers of social problems while ensuring that the venture is financially sustainable.

3.1.8 The Indian Startup Ecosystem: An Overview.

India: Statistics:

- Ranking: India has one of the largest startup ecosystems in the world and has more than 140,000 registered startups as of the middle of 2024.
- Growth Rate: The ecosystem is expanding at an annual rate of about 12-15%.
- Unicorns: More than 105 unicorns have been created in India, and new ones are popping up every day.

Major Growth Engines:
1. Digital Infrastructure: The acceleration of the startup growth rate is due to the widespread adoption of digital payment systems like UPI and low-cost data access.

2. Government Initiatives: Essential support is provided to entrepreneurs through programs like the Startup India, Stand Up India, and Atal Innovation Mission.
3. Funding and Investment: There has been a 15x increase in total startup funding due to increased investor participation.

Challenges and Opportunities:
- Scaling Issues: Almost 90% of the startups run into issues related to scaling, which is a major reason for the high failure rates within the first five years.
- Innovation Gaps: The problem is that India's deep tech innovation sector lags because of lower R&D investments.
- Regional Expansion: Nearly half of the startups in India are from Tier 2 and Tier 3 cities, which indicates the broader entrepreneurial growth.

Future Prospects:
- Job Creation: The economy has been greatly affected by the creation of more than 1.3 million jobs by the startups.
- Growth Potential: India can fast-track its economic growth by integrating education, entrepreneurship, and employment strategies.

The startup ecosystem in India is still growing and developing with the help of digitalization, government support, and a good investment climate. Removing the barriers to scalability and innovation will be essential for the long-term sustainability of the strategy.

3.1.9 Stages in the Startup Lifecycle

Pre-seed Stage:

The focus: Idea generation, market analysis and the formation of the team.

Key Activities: Verification of the concept, team generation, and initial research.

Seed Stage:

The focus: Developing the product, checking its viability in the market and obtaining early funding.

Key Activities: Developing the MVP, using it with initial users, and raising seed investment.

Early Stage (Startup Phase):

The focus: Refining the product, acquiring customers, and validating the business model.

Key Activities: Launch, analyse the feedback, and grow the team.

Growth Stage:

The focus: Developing operations, expanding market presence and obtaining Series B and C funding.

Key Activities: Business growth, enhance marketing and obtain larger funding.

Established Stage:

The focus: Sustainable profitability and operational efficiency.

Key Activities: Develop market position, improve processes, and attract talent.

Expansion Stage:

The focus: New markets and product lines.

Key Activities: Penetration of markets, new product development and formation of strategic alliances.

The focus: Long-term viability of the business and the strategies for the exit.

Key Activities: Financial management, considering mergers, and planning for the future.

The maturity/exit stage (exit phase):

The focus: Mergers and Acquisitions, or Initial Public Offering (IPO).

Key Activities: Finalization of the financials, best negotiations with the buyer or investor, and exit management.

Each of the startup stages is accompanied by its set of problems and promises that need careful planning and flexibility to ensure lasting success.

4.   Two channels to start a Proprietorship Company:

After working in a firm for one year, the employee can resign and become a Free Lancer to promote the previous parent company and there is no need to get GST since, he/she promoting the product of the parent company where he/she worked previously. In this mode of operation there is no need of GST. But, you cannot raise invoice and your company name cannot become a reference. Especially, Medical equipment will move depending on word of mouth from the existing customers (Doctors, Surgeons).

The other channel is taking sub dealership from the parent company and move the product in his/her company name. By doing so, your company name comes established and you will become reference.

For both the channel, giving good servicing support will give you good sales.

5. Ten Essential Steps for A Business Start-Up :

Beginning a business requires several, detailed steps such as undergoing research, preparing finance, and dealing with legal obligations. An organized approach often leads to a positive outcome.

5.1 Market Research:

Do Research on The Market Information about the market is necessary, especially if you want to start a business. Analyzing the market assists in pinpointing potential needs, evaluating rivals, and looking at the growth of the industries. This enables businesses to formulate a business strategy.

Points to Note:
- Understanding Demand: Figure out if there actually is a need for the good or service you are selling.
- Assessing Market Size: Attempt to find out how many people will be served by the goods or service you are offering.
- Analyzing Economic Trends: Look into checks such as the average wage in your target area and the employment rate. Choosing The Right Location: Figure out where your prospective market is located. Reviewing Competition: Examine the businesses that operate within your area of concern and have similar products or services.
- Setting Competitive Pricing: This requires checking the market rates and setting a charge. Example: Monitoring Prediction of Blood Pressure for Dialysis Patients. It is necessary to do thorough market research prior to introducing a device designed to monitor blood pressure changes during dialysis. Dialysis machines do not offer this feature, therefore extensive research and understanding of incorporated Healthcare policies and regulations for medical devices on the market is mandated.
- Market Need: Creating a system that can predict changes in blood pressure throughout dialysis is vital to improve

patient safety, therefore, innovation in this area would be invaluable.

- Potential Buyers: With the purchase of the device, hospitals and other dialysis centers and medical facilities are expected to become willing clients.
- Financial Aspects: Medical care organizations expect improved patient care with investment towards advanced medical equipment and devices which boosts the opportunity for adoption.
- Best Locations for Sales: This includes specialized medical colleges and hospitals, as well as the specialized centers of dialysis which are most likely to lead the new market.
- Industry Competition: If competition comes from a large medical equipment company that already has as similar product, then it will increase competition. On the other hand, there is a strong factor in the opposite direction, in that many vendors of dialysis machines already have the expensive machines, and replacing them or upgrading them, is costly. This BP prediction device comes under BLUE OCEAN STRATEGY. Economically, there seems to be an attractive alternative to these expensive machines which is a cheaper device.
- Pricing Strategy: To purchase the predictive device, you will need to find a balance between the cost of upgrading the old machines to be able to predict, or replacing them with completely new ones and setting a competitive price.

5.2 Create your business plan:

Your business plan forms the basis of your company. It serves as a guide to structure, operate, and expand your new venture. You'll employ it to persuade others that collaborating with you — or putting money into your company — makes good sense.

Find out more about crafting your business plan Business Plans come in two varieties:

A. Traditional Business Plan and

B. Lean Business Plan Lean startup style.

You might opt for a lean startup style if you need to explain or launch your business , your company is straightforward, or you intend to modify and polish your business plan often.

Lean startup styles use charts that include just a few elements to describe your company's value offer, structure, customers, and finances. They help you see trade-offs and key facts about your company . You can develop a lean startup template in various ways. A web search can lead you to free templates for building your business plan. Here, we talk about nine parts of a model business plan: Key partnerships Think about the other businesses or services you'll team up with to run your operation. Consider suppliers, manufacturers, subcontractors, and other strategic allies.

As I mentioned, you can have Stars, Cash Cows, Dogs and Question Marks to manage the company . Put your energy into Consumables for the capital equipment to sell, which will handle Conveyance and per diem costs. Key activities Jot down the ways your business will stand out from the competition. Highlight things like selling straight to customers, or using tech to tap into the sharing economy. The main task should be to service Medical Equipment so the customer (Doctor) feels confident your company will handle repairs when breakdowns happen.

Key resources Make a list of any resources you'll use to create value for your customer. Your most valuable assets might include staff, money, or intellectual property. Remember to use business resources that could be available to women, veterans,

Native Americans, and HUBZone businesses. Focus on extending the Annual Maintenance Contract at no cost for an extra year or two. This builds the Customer's trust in your company.

5.3 Value Proposition:

Our solution focuses on predicting blood pressure fluctuations during dialysis, ensuring patient safety by preventing dangerous episodes of hypo- and hypertension.

5.4 Customer Relationships:

Previously, customer interactions relied on cold calls. However, the approach has shifted towards digital engagement, where inquiries now come through online platforms. A visually appealing and informative company website is essential. Potential customers are influenced by detailed product explanations and recommendations from existing users.

5.5 Customer Segments:

Our primary target audience includes nephrologists and hospital executives who seek advanced blood pressure monitoring solutions during dialysis.

Additionally, companies specializing in blood pressure monitoring products will be industry competitors

5.6 Channels:

Effective customer communication involves multiple touchpoints. Once an inquiry is received through the website, the next step is to reach out via phone, schedule an appointment, and provide a product demonstration through Google Meet.

5.7 Cost Structure:

Our business strategy focuses on balancing cost efficiency with value maximization.

To determine profitability, we account for service constraints and the inclusion of a free extended maintenance contract while calculating the profit percentage.

5.8 Revenue Streams:

Our company generates revenue through direct sales, ensuring sustainable growth.

Key revenue sources include:

For Example:

1. Selling hardware for blood pressure prediction during dialysis.
2. Selling software designed for lung cancer prediction using CT scan images.

5.9 Financing of your business:

A business plan helps to estimate the capital required to start and maintain the company. If you have a lack of necessary funds, you may need to secure financing through personal savings, investors or loans. Different financing options exist depending on your financial condition and business goals.

5.9.1 Self -financing (bootstrapping):

Self -financing allows you to use your personal finances to start your business. This may include savings, financial assistance from family and friends or credit cards. The main advantage of self -financing is to maintain complete control over your business decisions. However, this also means taking all financial risks. It is important to avoid saving pensions, especially to avoid pensions, especially to avoid reducing the necessary money.

5.9.2 Venture Capital Investment :

The initiative provides funding from investors in exchange for partial ownership of the capital business. Unlike traditional loans, these funds do not require a refund, but investors will expect shares in the company.

5.9.3 Big points about Enterprise Capital:

Most suitable for companies with high growth capacity.

Investors provide capital in exchange for equity, not as a loan. Venture capitalists take high risk in expecting adequate returns.

These investments are long -lasting and may include active participation in business decisions. Most investors will play a role in leading the company and can ask for a seat on the board. If you choose this option, you must be ready to share some control over business.

5.9.4 How to get risk capital financing:

There is no guaranteed way to obtain business capital, but the process usually follows a standard order of basic stages.

1. Search an investor Look for individual investors - sometimes "angel investors" or venture capital companies.
2. To find out enough background research to ensure whether the investor is excreted and works with start - up companies.
3. Share your business plan: The investor will review your business plan to ensure that it meets their investment criteria. Most investment funds focus on the phase of
4. an industry, geographical area or business development.
5. Go through the correct work review Investors will look at the company's management team, markets, products and services, corporate administration documents and accounting.
6. Full conditions: If they want to invest, the next step is to agree on a schedule that describes the terms and conditions of funds to invest. Investment: When you agree

with a schedule, you can get investments! When a venture fund has invested, it is actively registering in the company. Venture funds normally come in the "round". When the company meets milestones, the financing of the further rounds performs available, the company carries out its plan with the price adjustment. Use crowdfunding to fund your business Crowdfunding raises funds for a business with a large number of people, called crowdfunders. Crowdfunders usually do not get a proportion of ownership of the business and do not expect financial return on their money. Instead, crowdfunders are expected to receive "gifts" from your company, because thanks to their contribution. Often the gift is the product you are planning or planning other special quotas, such as meeting the owner of the business or getting their name in credit. This crowdfunding creates a popular choice for those who want to produce creative features (such as a documentary), or a physical product (eg high -tech cooler). Crowdfunding is also popular, as it is very low for business owners. Not only do you have to maintain full control of your company, but if your plan fails, you usually have no compulsion to repay Crowdfunders. Each crowdfunding platform is different, so be sure to read the nice print and understand your complete financial and legal obligations. Examples: There are quarantine conversion from the reality music show in Tamil Nadu in the Corona period. Conducted by Mrs. Subashree Thanigachalam.

7. Get a small business loan If you want to maintain full control of your business but do not have enough money to start, consider a small business loan. To increase the possibility of acquiring loans, you must have a business plan, expenditure sheet and financial estimate over the next five years. These devices will guess how much you need to ask, and will help the bank know that they are making a smart alternative by giving you a loan. Once you have prepared the content, you can contact banks and credit associations to request the loan. You will compare the offer to get the best possible conditions for your loan. MSME in India provides loans and with grants. In the later

phase, we will discuss the financing agencies in India in detail. Choose your business location Your business site is one of the most important decisions you make. Originally if no showroom is needed, you can do yourself as a factory in the industrial area and the marketing office in your home. The options you make can affect the tax, legal requirements and revenues. Learn more about choosing business space

5.10 Choose a business structure:

The legal structure you chose for your business will affect business registration requirements, how much you pay in tax and your personal responsibility. Your professional structure affects how much you pay in taxes, your ability to raise money, paperwork you have and your personal responsibility. You must choose a business structure before registering your business in the state. Most companies must also receive a tax number and archive for the correct license and permission. Choose carefully. When you can turn into a separate business structure in the future, there may be restrictions based on your location. This can also lead to tax outcomes and unexpected resolution among other complications.

Consultation with professional consultants, lawyers and accountants can prove to be useful.

Single ownership: It is easy to create a single ownership and give you full control of your business. If you do business activities, you are automatically considered the only ownership but not registered as any other type of business. The only ownership does not produce its own business unit. This means that your commercial property and obligations are not different from your personal property and obligations. You may be held personally responsible for business loans and obligations.

5.10.1 Partnership:

A partnership is a simple business structure in which two or more people share ownership. There are two main types : Limited Partnership (LPS) and Limited Liability Partnership (LLPS). ,, - Limited Partnership (LPS) : At least one general partner with unlimited responsibility, while other partners have minimal control over limited responsibility and operations as mentioned in a partnership agreement. The profits undergo individual tax returns, and the general partner will also have to pay taxes with self -employed persons. - ** Limited Liability Partnership (LLPS) ** All partners provide liability protection, and ensure that no persons are responsible for business loans or other partners. Partnership is ideal for multi -owner companies, professional groups (for example, laws or accounting firms), and entrepreneurs formally test formally a business idea. ### ** Limited Liabilities Company (LLC) . A LLC combines the characteristics of both partnerships and companies, and offers obligations conservation while maintaining tax flexibility. - The owners' individual properties (for example home and savings) are usually protected from commercial obligations. - Profits and disadvantages undergo personal income without corporate tax, even though LLC members have to pay self-employed taxes for medicines and social security. - Some states require LLC, until ownership is changed until an operating agreement otherwise specifies. LLCs are best suited for companies with high risks, which are very risk, and demanding wealth protection for owners, and who want to reduce taxes than companies.

5.10.2 Private Limited Company:

You can register a Start Up under Private Limited Company. But it has greater Complaince. To maintain you have to spend some cumulative amount to the Auditor apart from paying rent and maintenance to Incubation Center.

6. Steps needed to set up your business:

Step 1: Choosing the right business name

Your business name is a big part of your brand. It should be unique, easy to remember and related to the concept of the business. You can verify if the name is available for use before finalizing it to avoid legal issues.

Step 2: To make sure your business is legally recognized

Directly after selecting a name, you need to ensure that your business is registered in order to be legally recognized. If your business is operating under a name different from your own, you may require registration with relevant authorities (state) may be required. This step makes your business official and offers legal protections.

Step 3: Get tax identity number (tin)

A TIN or EIN is a tax identification number that is used in handling taxes, hiring employees and opening business bank accounts. You should check with your state as there may be additional requirements for some states based on local tax laws.

Step 4: Get professional license and permission

To operate legally, one must have the right license and permission dependenting on the industry and location. Not all countries are the same and some industries for example, health and food have very specific rules. For instance, companies that deal with medical equipment need special licensing.

Step 5: Open business bank account

A commercial bank account is a separate account that holds the individual's finance and the company's finance separately to make tax submission and financial management easier.

If you are planning to start a proprietor company (example in medical electronics fields), it is advisable to gain industry experience first. The first year can be less risky by working with dealer companies. In India, medical electronic business dealers are common and it is therefore advantageous to begin as a sales or service engineer in a core medical electronics company.

This will help you gain in-depth product knowledge and market experience.

When you know the products, you can freelance as a negotiator for the same company as the single point of entry. Since you already know the product, it will be easier to market and sell it under your own business name. To legally operate, you need to obtain a GST number and the sales license from the government of India.

In order to establish your business, the following is required:

 - a registered office address (your home can be used in the first instance)
* a two -wheeler for travel
* a mobile phone
* a computer with internet connection
* a corporate website for marketing

Your ability to cover a particular geographical area will determine the sales limit. In general, a daily operating radius of about 80 km is considered manageable. To establish your customer base, your original parent company should basically provide leads which helps you to close sales effectively.

<u>Sales strategy for customer commitment:</u>

A structured sales method is important. Limit the call with a potential customer to 3 calls , to customize time and effort: First conversation - recognize the customers' ability and interest. Other conversation - explain the technical aspects and benefits of the product. Third call - Complete the sale and secure payment (via demand draft or through online transfer such as GPAY).

Seller on Amazon: Another viable route is to take advantage of e-commerce platforms such as Amazon to sell medical electronic products online. This eliminates geographical boundaries and allows you to tap on a comprehensive customer base.

However, selling online requires efficient product list, branding and digital marketing strategies.

7. How to generate revenue for the Proprietorship company:

Classification of medical electronic products in an ownership business Medical electronic products can be classified using a well -known business analysis structure, BCG Matrix (Boston Consulting Group Matrix). This model classifies products based on market growth rate and market share, allowing companies to prioritize their focus areas effectively.

The stars will generate revenue once at a time. But with great benefits. To run a company and better meet marketing costs for 2 or 3 cash cows. For example, for ultrasound and lung function test machines in cash such as cows. The benefits you receive will be enough to meet convention expenses and for your salary. To begin with, you must act as a OFFICE BOY to CEO of your ownership ship company. Don't focus on dogs to begin with. Focus on question marks and AI and ml in this category. Now a revolution will be such that all our next generation of medical equipment will be accompanied by the application of AI and ML.

8. How and when to convert the holder company to a start -up company:

When your bank is sufficient to take care of a balance visor, you can go to start up, which closes the operation of the holder ship company to satisfy compliance.

When you go back during your college days based on your project, you can participate in Idea Hakathon (II and III years), and by winning the price you can start a start -up. Or by getting seed fund also you can initiate Start Up. When you get out of college, the prototype of the product should be prepared and you need to get bootstraping Fund/ Angel Investor/ Venture Capitalist Fund as the case may be.

9. How to generate revenue for the startup company:

The revenues generated when it is proprietorship company should support salary, conversion and auditor fees, etc., then you should apply for various nodal

financing agencies for developing prototypes and present various investors through incubators and to various nodal financing agencies such as Birac (BIG FUND), Nidhi Prayas, Nidhi Ayas. The main component of a bootstraped Finance Pitch Deck:

1. Company name and logo - Contact information (city, e - mail, phone number) – URL
2. A card of the concept, product or service but informative observation
3. Corporate overview - Mission, vision and main value that defines the company's purpose
4. Problem declaration is supported by relevant data or

examples, emphasizes your boot address

5. The solution indicates how your product or service effectively solves the problem, highlights its unique characteristics.
6. Team - Members of the leading team show their expertise and experience - Important advisors or strategic partners providing guidance and assistance
7. Market analysis - Identifying the target market including customer segments, their needs and market capacity
8. For example if we consider Medical Equipment Business, Medical Colleges and Hospitals will be our Target Segment 8 Competitive landscape, details of competitors and unique benefits of your start -up
9. If you consider Blood Pressure Prediction during Dialysis all BP apparatus manufacturers will become Competitors.
10. Business Model - Explain how your start -up generates revenue, ensures scalability and prolonged stability
11. Marketing and Sales Strategy - Strategies to attract and maintain customers - Cost to get customers and their estimated lifetime value
12. Economic estimates - Expected revenue, expenses and break-even analysis to provide insight into economic growth capacity
13. Milestones - Future goals and roadmaps for expansion of the company
14. Evaluation and Investment Request Suggested : Assessment for Funding Round Future capital requirements and financial planning
15. Exit strategy: Possible output options for investors such as procurement, fusion or public offer
16. Call for action: A compelling end statement encourages investors to take the next step Explicit details how they can associate further.

By integrating these components, pitch will effectively show the start -up capacity and attract the right investment opportunities.

10. License for construction/ imported medical equipment in India:

Here, with the classification of medical equipment, the license required to sell, produce and import medical equipment in India has been observed. To sell medical equipment, you usually need a wholesale medication license if you work with classified medical equipment in the form of medicines. However, for medical equipment that is not classified as medicines, specific license requirements may vary depending on the type and classification of the device. In general, a wholesale license for medical equipment is not clearly mentioned, but compliance with CDSCO rules is necessary.

10.1 License required for the construction of medical equipment:

To produce medical equipment in India, you need CDSCO production license. The license is issued by the Standards Control Organization (CDSCO) for the central substance under the CLAA scheme. The process involves submitting a comprehensive application, including form 27, and to ensure compliance with guidelines for good production practices (GMP)
.

10.2 License required to import medical equipment:

To import medical equipment into India, you need the MD -15 license. The license is issued by the Central Licensing Authority (CLA) after submitting an application in Form MD -14. The license is usually valid for three years and then requires renewal. Classification of medical equipment Medical equipment in India is classified in four categories based on their risk level: • Class A: Low risk equipment, such as tongue presses and straps. • Class B:

At least moderate risk units, such as glue. • Class C: Medium - T - Garden Risk Device, such as Pacemaker. • Class D: High risk equipment, such as heart valve 24.

This classification determines specific government requirements and approval process for each unit.

11. Import Export Code:

Import export code (IEC) is a unique 10-innovative code issued by Director General for Foreign Trade in India. It is compulsory for companies involved in imports or export activities.

How to apply for importer expiry code (IEC):
1. Access the DGFT portal: Go to the DGFT website and create a user account.
2. Fill the application: Fill in the IEC application form with the required details.
3. Upload the document: Upload scanned copies of the required documents.
4. Payment fee: Use online payment port to pay the current fee.
5. Submit the application: Submit the form and wait for confirmation.
6. Get IEC: In case of successful verification, the IEC code will be released and e -posted. Documents required for IEC registration:
   - PAN CARD: Permanent account number (PAN) A copy of the card.
   - Evidence of identity: Aadhaar card, passport or selects -D for owners.
   - Evidence of address: Sales act, rental agreement, leases, electricity bills, etc.
   - Bank details: Evidence of bank account in the company's name (eg interrupted check, bank certificate).

- Digital Signature Certificate (DSC): For online submission.
- Law of government: If applicable

Note: IEC code is now connected to PAN number, but it is still released separately by DGFT

12. Pitching to the Investors:

Once you have decided to raise funds from potential investors, the path should focus On the following: - Identification pain point - verification from the clinical team - Minimum viable products (MVP) - Unique sales point for your product (USP) - Discrimination from competition - Total Available Market (TAM) - business plan - 1, 3 and 5 years - return on the investment Team Building - Street On The Street (foot) - Development area - Product, Sales Team, Customer Help And Seek Money.

1. Crowdfunding : Offer prizes, equity or debt -based incentives on the basis of platform.
2. Prepare a compelling pitch and exploit social media to reach potential supporters.
3. Venture Capital (VC) : See VC companies if your start - up has high growth capacity.
4. Prepare a strong pitch and research companies that match your industry.
5. Be prepared to interact on equity and conditions, as VCs often play an active role in directing start -up.
6. Angelinvestor : Look for individual investors delivering capital in exchange for equity or convertible loans. Use Angel Network or online platforms to contact potential investors.
7. Boot accelerator and incubator .

13. Pitching to the Competitions:

- Participate in competitions where you present your views to win funding or get investor exposure.
- Even if you do not win, these events can help you make valuable connections

Pre -sale : Sell your product or service before launching funds to generate funds and validate market demand.

1. Business participation : Partners with companies that match your goals. Many people run incubators, demo days or innovation programs. To ensure such partnership: Create a minimum viable product (MVP) and a large - scale network.
2. Equity Crowdfunding: Provide the company's partial ownership.This method allows the extensive groups of investors to contribute when sharing risk
3. Friend and family: Look for initial money from your personal network. This is often the fastest way to raise small amounts of capital, but clear agreements are required to avoid conflicts.

14. Necessary legal documents for a Start Up:

1. The Memorandum of Association (MOA): This document emphasizes the company's goals, business activities, authorized share capital and responsibility for the members.
2. Association's Articles (AOA): A user for the company acts as a manual, describes the guidelines for internal governance and operations, including shareholder rights and director.
3. Incorporation certificate: was issued by the Register of Companies, who confirmed the legal existence of the company and allowed to be operated on as a separate unit.
4. 4th Director Identification Number (DIN): Each company is required to submit official documents.
5. 5. Permanent account number (PAN): Required for financial transactions and tax submission.

Registration and license

1. Registration of goods and services (GST): Required for companies with more turnover than GST threshold.
2. Trademark registration: The boot mark protects the identity and intellectual property.
3. Digital Signature Certificate (DSC): Required for electronic submission at the Ministry of Corporate Affairs.

Agreement and contract

1. Shareholder agreement: Defines the rights and responsibilities of shareholders.
2. Co -founder agreement: Equity emphasizes owners' investment, investment and responsibilities.
3. Non-complication agreement (NDAS): Confidential information shared with partners or staff security measures.

Compliance and reporting

1. Start -up India Registration: Provides benefits such as tax exemption and simplified compliance processes.
2. Regular submission to MCA: Necessary to maintain active status and compliance with the Companies Act.
3. By completing these legal formalities, Startups can ensure that they work within the legal framework and maintain a strong base for development and success.

15. A corporation partnership (LLP):

It is a commercial structure that combines the benefits of partnership with the responsibility of a company. There is a separate legal unit that is different from the partners, so that it can allow its own property, enter the contracts and is independently subject to legal obligations.

15.1 Important features in an LLP:

- Limited liability: Partners have limited personal responsibility, which means that their property is protected from business loans and obligations. Each partner is only responsible to the extent that the investment in LLP.
- Flexibility in management: Partners can actively participate in business management, and the nuances of operation and gain distribution are determined by an adaptable agreement between partners.
- Separate Legal Unit: An LLP is recognized as a separate legal entity similar to a company, which increases the reliability of stakeholders.
- Minimum two partners: At least two partners need to create an LLP, without the upper limit for the number of partners.
- Nominated partners: At least two designated partners in an LLP shall be responsible for compliance with regulations,

with a country resident (in the case of india)

15.2 Cost and compliance in LLP:

Limited Liability Participation (LLP) offers low formation costs and low regulatory requirements than private limited companies, making them easier to manage.

15.3 The benefits of llp

- Protection of limited liability: Partner's personal property is safe against business risk.
- Operating flexibility: Partners have the freedom to control the business without excessive limitations.
- Tax benefits: LLP is often regarded as implementation institutions, which prevent double taxation.
- Due to their structural and operational flexibility, LLPS is particularly preferred by professional service companies such as laws and accounting firms.

15.4 Big differences between a partnership and an LLP

Responsibility

Partnership: Partners have unlimited personal responsibility for trade loans and obligations, and put their personal property at risk.

LLP: Partner's responsibility is limited to their investment in LLP, which ensures individual asset protection.

Legal status

Partnership: Not considered a separate legal entity; This is an extension of the partners themselves.

LLP: Recognized as a separate legal entity, separated from the partners, makes it possible to enter into contracts and sues the case independently.

Formation and registration

Partnership: Registration is optional according to the Indian Participation Act, 1932.

LLP: Registration is mandatory according to Limited Liability Participation Act, 2008.

Administer

Partnership: All partners usually share management responsibility.

LLP: Specific partners are nominated to handle business operations.

Continuity

Partnership: The company is dissolved whether a partner's death or back to an otherwise in an agreement.

LLP: This exists regardless of changes in partnership, and ensures trade continuity.

LLP: Even when you change your partner, it exists.

15.5 Taxation

- Partnership: Partners pay personal income tax from their part of the profits. Partnership is not taxed as a separate unit
- LLP: Considered a separate legal unit for tax fairs, but partners are only charged tax on income they receive from LLP

15.6 Compliance

- Partnership: compliance with low regulator
- LLP: More regulatory compliance, including annual submission of accounts and returns with the Register of Companies.

15.7 Ownership and property

- Partnership: Property is jointly owned by partners.
- LLP: The assets themselves are owned by LLP, which is independent of partners.

15.8 Maximum number of partners

- Partnership: Limited to 100 partners.
- LLP: No limit on number of partners

15.9 Foreign participation

- Partnership: Foreign citizens cannot form a partnership company in India
- LLP: Foreign citizens can create an LLP with an Indian resident

15.10. Benefits of LLP compared to a traditional Partnership Company

Here are the benefits of a corporation (LLP) compared to a traditional partnership company:

The benefits of LLP:

15.10.1. Limited liability:

- In an LLP, partners have limited liability, which means that their personal property is preserved in the business or obligations.
- This is a significant advantage of traditional participation where partners are individually responsible for all commercial loans

15.10.2. Flexibility in management and ownership:

- LLPs provide flexibility in handling ownership of business and structure so that partners can define their roles and profit sharing according to their agreement
- Unlike companies, LLP is not bound by strict statutory rules for internal governance.

15.10.3. Tax Benefits:

- LLP is taxed as a partnership, which means that the business does not pay taxes; Instead, profits and disadvantages are reported on the part's individual tax returns.
- LLPS has no dividend distribution fee (DDT), which is beneficial to partners

15.10.4. Increase in reliability:

- LLP has its own legal identity and is registered with government officials and increases their credibility and investment goals.
- This openness and formal registration make LLP more attractive to investors and lenders.

15.10.5. Easy incorporation and compliance:

- The process of incorporating an LLP is relatively simple and cost compared to other commercial structures such as private limited companies.
- LLP requires low compliance, such as submission of annual returns and accounts, which reduces operating costs

15.10. 6. No minimum capital required:

- There is no need for minimum capital contribution to create an LLP, providing partners flexibility

15.10.7 Comparison with traditional partnership companies

- Responsibility: Traditional participation does not offer protection of limited responsibilities and risks the partners' individual properties.
- Flexibility and reliability: LLP provides more flexibility in management and is seen as more reliable because of their formal registration.
- Taxation: Both LLP and traditional partnerships are equally taxed, but LLP avoids double taxation.
- Correction process: LLP has a streamlined incorporation process compared to traditional participation, which often involves more informal agreements.

Overall, the LLP partnership operates with limited responsibility with flexibility, making them an attractive alternative for many businesses.

16. Limitations with limited liability

Limited Liability Partnership (LLP) and partnership companies have their own sets of boundaries. Here are some big limits for each:

1. Limited development opportunities: LLP -er cannot issue shares to the public, which limits their ability to raise large amounts of capital from investors.
2. Limited recognition: LLP is not recognized as private limited companies, making it difficult to raise money from investors.
3. Requirements for compliance: LLP shall follow various statutory requirements, such as submission of annual returns and maintenance of accounts for accounts
4. Protection of limited liability: While LLPs provide protection of limited liability, individual property may be at risk if a partner engages in fraudulent activities or fails to follow the LLP agreement
5. Limited lifetime: an LLP is dissolved when some partners' death, retirement or insolvency, affecting long -lasting stability
6. Difficulty with ownership transfer: Ownership rights are not easily transferable without the consent of all partners taxation and llps -restrictions
7. LLP -er is subject to higher tax rates than other commercial institutions, making the taxation an important idea for entrepreneurs.

Challenges from a partnership company

1. Unlimited liability: Partners are individually responsible for business loans, and put their personal property at risk.
2. Limited flexibility: Participation provides less management and ownership flexibility than LLP or companies.
3. No separate legal entity: Since a partnership is not different from the partners, legal and financial conditions can be complicated.
4. Limited access to capital: Participation depends on personal savings or loans for money, as they cannot issue shares as companies.
5. Discolor: A partnership can be dissolved if a partner leaves, unless specific provisions are involved in the partnership agreement.

17. LLP vs Partnership - A comparison

LLPs provide benefits with limited responsibilities, protect individual property, but they may have obstacles to scaling and wealth. On the other hand, participation provides operational flexibility, but exposes partners to unlimited personal responsibility.

18. Requirements for compliance for LLPS

Greater compliance obligations:

1. LLP agreement Submission: LLP Agreement shall be presented within 30 days of incorporation using form -3.
2. Annual submission of return (form -11): Management and ownership shall be archived by May 30 each year.
3. Description and solvency description (form -8): An economic summary will be presented by an annual 30

October.
4. Income tax (ITR-5): July 31 (or September 30 when revised) should be filed.
5. GST registration: If the annual turnover is more than £ 40 lakh for goods or more than £ 20 lakh for sight
6. Statutory audit: mainly if turnover is more than £ 40 lakh or capital contribution is more than £ 25 lakhs

19. The benefits of Compliance:

- Increases reliability and legal status.
- Penal and legal issues are avoided.
- Provides tax benefits

Penalty for non-transport:

- Failure to archive form 11 attracts a fine of 100 per day.
- Delay in the submission of the LLP agreement, which imposes 100 per day per day without any roof.

20. Start Up companies' Compliance :

Start-up companies, often structured as private limited companies, have more complex requirements for compliance than LLP. Great requirements include:

1. Annual submission of return: With the registrar (ROC) of file form MGT-7 and Form AOC-4 companies.
2. Submission of financial description: File revised accounts with ROC.
3. Income tax: If you are revised, you will submit IR - 6 by September 30.
4. GST Registration: If the annual turnover is £ 40 Lakh for goods or more than £ 20 lakh for services.
5. Tax deduction and collection: Get a tax deduction account number (TAN) for tax claims.

The benefits of compliance:

- Ensures legal security and reliability.
- Provides access to financing and investment.
- Legal punishment and punishment are avoided

Penalty for non-transport:

- Failure to submit annual returns and accounts can lead to fine and legal steps.
- GST and income tax rules along with non-fasting result in penalties and interest tax

In summary, while LLP has less requirements for compliance than private limited companies, both structures must follow specific legal and financial obligations to maintain their operational validity and avoid punishment.

21. Make in India:

The growth of the production sector introduced by Prime Minister Narendra Modi in September 2014 aims to position India as a global production power plant. The programme hopes to expand investment opportunities, promote innovation, develop a qualified workforce, and improve infrastructure to support industry growth. Skills that provide employees with training to meet industry development requirements. Efforts have been made to simplify regulations and streamline business processes to improve simple business operations. Some of the most important sectors that will benefit from this initiative are:

- Automobile and autocomponents Aerospace and defense manufacturing
- Information Technology and IT-enabled Services (ITES)
- Renewable Energy

From 2023 to 2024, the proportion of GDP sectors remains lower than expected.

To strengthen domestic production, the government has introduced a Production Incentive (PLI) scheme and ordered 1.97 lakh crore rupees, which exceeds 14 key sectors, to improve production and exports. However, challenges such as infrastructure limitations and complexity of regulatory effects continue to affect progress. The most important highlights are:

22. Financial Support for Startups

The Startup Growth Fund was sent for startup capital with registered investment channels. (AI), quantum computing and semiconductor research. To strengthen private sector F&E concentration, 20,000 crores have been allocated to technology-driven innovation. Government commitment to establish a strong, innovation-driven startup ecosystem in India to ensure better access to funds and resources.

23. Startup India Seed Fund Scheme (SFSFS)

The Startup India Seed Fund Scheme is intended to help early-stage startups develop and commercialize ideas. Prototype development and up to ¹50 lakh for scaling operations via convertible equipment. Founder Market enthusiasm helps startups improve their product market and is more appealing to investors.

The Startup India Seed Finance Conspire (SISFS) could be a government-backed activity outlined to supply budgetary help to early-stage new companies in India.

Here are key points of interest around the scheme:

Overview of the Startup India Seed Support Scheme

Objective: The conspire points to back new companies in their early stages, centering on confirmation of concept, model advancement, item trials, advertise section, and commercialization

Funding: It offers up to 20 lakh crore rupees as a give for model improvement and up to 50 lakh for showcase section and scaling through convertible debentures or debt-linked instruments

Eligibility: New businesses must be recognized by DPIIT and joined inside the final two a long time. They ought to utilize innovation in their center item or benefit and have a reasonable business idea with potential for scaling.

<u>Benefits of the Scheme</u>

- Non -Dilutive Financing: Gifts don't require value weakening, decreasing monetary hazard for founders
- Market Approval: Bolsters new companies in accomplishing product-market fit
- Investor Certainty: Securing seed subsidizing makes new businesses more alluring to wander capitalists and blessed messenger investor
- Mentorship & Organizing: Numerous seed financing programs offer master direction and organizing opportunities

<u>Application Process</u>

Application Entrance: New businesses can apply online through the official Startup India portal

Incubator Part: Financing is dispensed through qualified hatcheries over India

Other Seed Subsidizing Options

In expansion to the Startup India Seed Support Conspire, new businesses can investigate other seed financing choices such as:

Angel Financial specialists: Give seed cash in trade for value and offer mentorship

Venture Capitalists: A few VCs specialize in equity- based seed financing for early-stage startups

Crowdfunding Stages: Permit new businesses to raise reserves from people in trade for early item get to or rewards

Business Hatcheries & Quickening agents: Offer seed financing, mentorship, and organizing openings in trade for a little value stake

24. Blessed messenger speculators and wander capitalists (VCs):

They are both vital sources of subsidizing for new businesses, but they contrast in their approach, financing sums, and association. Here's a breakdown of the key differences:

1. Source of Funds

Angel Speculators: Utilize their claim cash to contribute in new businesses. They are ordinarily affluent people looking for high-risk, high-reward opportunities

Venture Capitalists: Contribute pooled reserves from teach, enterprises, or well off people. They oversee these reserves professionally as portion of a wander capital firm

2. Speculation Stage

Angel Speculators: Center on early-stage new businesses, regularly giving seed financing to assist businesses get off the ground

Venture Capitalists: Contribute in new companies at different stages, counting early development and afterward stages, with a inclination for companies appearing demonstrated adaptability and development potential

3. Speculation Size

Angel Financial specialists: Regularly contribute littler sums, extending from $25,000 to $100,000 separately or up to $1 million collectively when portion of a group1

Venture Capitalists: Contribute much bigger entireties, frequently beginning at $1 million and going up to $100 million or more

4. Involvement

Angel Investors: Generally less included within the business operations. They may offer exhortation or mentorship in case craved but are not committed to do so.

Venture Capitalists: Take an dynamic part within the company, giving key direction, making a difference with enrollment, and closely observing the business's execution to secure their investment

5.   Hazard Tolerance

Angel Financial specialists: More willing to require dangers on dubious thoughts since they contribute in new companies at their most punctual stages.

Venture Capitalists: Lean toward businesses with a few level of advertise approval and a clear path to versatility, lessening their hazard exposure

6.   Value and Control

Angel Financial specialists: Require value stakes but regularly don't request critical control over the business

Venture Capitalists: Frequently require bigger value stakes and may request a controlling intrigued or board seats to impact major choices

Summary table

Aspect	Angel Investors	Venture Capitalists
Funding Source	Personal funds from individuals	Capital collected from investment firms or funds
Investment Stage	Primarily early-stage startups	Ranges from early-stage to large- scale businesses
Typical Investment Amount	$20K– $1M	$1M– $100M+
Level of Involvement	Minimal involve ment, may offer mentorship	Actively involved in business strategy and decision- making
Risk Tolerance	Higher risk-taking willingness	More calculated risk approach
Equity & Control	Aquires a small stake	Larger ownership stake with greater influence on business operations

Both options provide crucial funding based on a startup's needs. Angel investors help businesses take off, while venture capitalists support growth and expansion

www.ingramcontent.com/pod-product-compliance
Lightning Source LLC
Chambersburg PA
CBHW020511160726
47991CB00007B/2896